I0479943

POOPER SCOOPER BUSINESS

How to Make $300 a Day Scooping Poop

TABLE OF CONTENTS

INTRODUCTION

The What and the Why

What if I told you that starting a business that earns a living, yet has minimal start-up costs, is possible? What if I said you could make up to $300 per day *just* scooping poop? Believe it or not, this is a real business option that many people are turning to—and making money from!

As of 2022, 70% of US households owned a pet. This is an astounding number of people willing to pay for services related to the upkeep of their furry family members. Starting a pooper scooper business is one way to capitalize on this industry and make money while doing something that you may actually enjoy.

Pet waste is a huge business, and to understand why it's vital to look at the facts. Nearly 69 million households in the United States own a pet dog, and 45.3 million have a cat. If you think those numbers are astounding, consider how much pet waste our furry friends generate annually.

According to the Environment Protection Agency, our favorite four-legged friends create three-quarters of a pound of waste daily. Altogether, that's over 25,000 tons of dog waste produced daily in the US, which doesn't include cats or other pets. Altogether, that comes to over 10 million tons of pet waste yearly.

This ultimately translates to an opportunity for you to create a business out of cleaning up after our furry friends. You can make a living by starting your own pooper scooper business, and all it takes is minimal start-up costs, some good old-fashioned work, and dedication.

Consider this, in 2021, the total pet industry generated over $123 billion. People really do enjoy spending money on their pet's needs, so why not make a business out of helping those who don't have time to do the dirty work themselves? With that said, the dog pet waste revenue generated was also no small figure. This alone came in at over $3.5 billion—a ton of money!

The job offers some great perks—you get to spend time outdoors, enjoy fresh air and exercise, and have a flexible schedule. Plus, making extra money is easy without needing qualifications or special skills. When it comes to waste management, you are the expert. You also have the freedom to find clients, set your pricing, and scale your business whenever you're ready to take it to the next level.

If you're concerned that you don't know where to begin and know little about building your own business, you can rest assured that this guide will provide the information necessary to make your pooper scooper business a success. You'll discover the earning potential, how to start up, what supplies to purchase, how to price services accordingly, and more. Let's get started!

EARNING POTENTIAL

One of the big questions on everyone's mind when considering starting up a pooper scooper business is how much money can you make? Fortunately, numerous sources back up the earning potential of running this type of business.

For instance, Business Insider covered an entrepreneur making $25,000 a month by scooping up after pets full-time. Many YouTubers believe earning anywhere from $800 to over $8,000 monthly is doable if you do the work. However, the ones making the most usually organize several workers and have a system in place for multiple services.

There are also franchise opportunities where you're given territory and existing clients. But what if you're new to the pet waste business? In that case, your earning might differ from someone with years of experience.

Glassdoor states that the average salary of someone working as a pet waste removal specialist is around $58,000 yearly, but many professionals earn much more. Generally speaking, the ability to make around $35 an hour with a complete book of clients at 40 hours per week is possible.

Of course, the amount you make will depend on the area you're located in and how many weekly or monthly services clients are looking for. For one-off clientele, earning $45 to $50 a visit is incredibly common. You can further maximize your income if you have repeat business and offer discounts, but we'll explain that later.

A typical price to charge nationwide for weekly or monthly cleans is around $25. This depends on several factors, such as how many pets a person has or the size of their yard. Considering these factors when setting your prices is essential, which we'll discuss in more detail later on.

No matter how much you make, one thing is for sure—this business can provide a steady income and great financial flexibility. Plus, the earning potential is huge if you eventually choose to scale up. A good milestone to aim for is $300 a day, broken down over 260 workdays, completing six one-off services daily, or twenty repeat customers daily.

That's achievable if you're willing to put in the effort and take advantage of all the opportunities around you. With a book of one hundred clients that purchase your services weekly, $300 is absolutely doable. But before posting ads and getting the word out, you must know how to start your business and what supplies to get. Let's take a look.

HOW TO START

The first step for any business is to select a name. Choosing the right name for your pooper scooper business will set you apart from competitors and give potential customers an idea of your services.

Your business name should be catchy, professional, and easy to remember. Consider incorporating keywords in your title such as "poop", "scoop", "pets," or "waste removal." You can also devise a humorous phrase that reflects your services, like "Poop Happens" or "Scoopy Doo."

What matters is that you're happy with your business name and confident it will make a good impression. Once you have chosen your business name, ensure it isn't already taken by conducting an online search. You should check business registration databases, domain name registrars, and social media handles to ensure the name is not taken.

Once you have your business name selected, it's time to register your business with the state. Depending on where you live, you will need a new or assumed business name filing, an employer identification number (EIN), and proof of business address. Registering your business will give you all the documentation needed to open a business bank account and apply for the necessary permits.

Now it's time to choose the type of business entity you prefer. The most popular entities are sole proprietorships, limited liability companies (LLCs), and corporations. Each has different advantages, so be sure to research them carefully before deciding.

The type of business entity you form also depends on where you live and the scope of your services. Sole proprietorships are simpler to set up, but limited liability companies (LLCs) offer more protection for personal assets if something goes wrong with the business. It's best to talk to an accountant or business attorney to decide the best option for you.

There are also corporations, but a sole proprietorship or LLC is likely the most suitable if you operate this business alone. There's a lot more paperwork and maintenance involved with a corporation, making it less ideal for a solo business. However, let's say that one day you want to franchise your business and expand into multiple locations—that's when a corporation makes more sense.

After registering your business, you must check whether any permits are required in your city or state. These can include licenses for pet waste removal, general business licenses, and permits for using commercial vehicles. While most people won't ask whether you're licensed, failing to receive state or city licenses for the pet waste removal you complete can result in costly fines and even legal charges. So, make sure to double-check the requirements for your area.

Once the paperwork is out of the way, it's time to get started on your branding materials. Create email addresses, social media accounts, and a website for your business. Generally, you can create an email address on the same sites you use to check your personal emails or use the email addresses that come with your website hosting package.

Hosting a website costs as little as $4 a month for a simple WordPress site, but you can also go with simpler options from service providers like Wix, Squarespace, and Weebly. If you don't feel comfortable with creating a website yourself, you can hire a web developer to do it for you. However, the service providers mentioned above all have easy webpage builders, so you won't need the expertise to get your website up and running.

Next, it would be best to consider getting some basic coverage with a business insurance policy in case of accidents. Many business insurance policies are designed specifically for pet waste removal companies. It will provide you with liability coverage, protecting your business if a customer makes a claim against it.

While you might think skipping insurance coverage is a way to reduce costs, it can be an expensive mistake if someone gets injured on the job. When visiting clients' homes and cleaning their yards, it's always better to be safe than sorry.

Lastly, you must open a business bank account to track your income and expenses. Most banks will require paperwork like EINs and articles of incorporation (if applicable). It's also essential that the name on the bank account matches precisely the one used for your business registration.

The easiest option is to create a business bank account at the branch where you already have a personal account. If you don't want to use the same bank, look for one that offers special discounts and benefits to small businesses. A favorable business bank history will be beneficial if you decide to apply for a loan or line of credit in the future.

By setting up your business correctly, you can ensure that all the essential matters are taken care of and that you're running a legitimate business. It's ideal to pay the slight costs to establish an official business entity in your state so that you can reap the rewards later. After you've completed these steps, you may consider finding an accountant, lawyer, and other professionals to help you keep your business running smoothly.

Now that you know the basics of how to start a pooper scooper business, you can begin building a brand and developing procedures for customer service. With dedication and hard work, it won't be long before customers come knocking on your door—and your finances will begin to flourish. Let's discuss the details, including the supplies you'll need and the steps to ensure success.

SUPPLIES TO START

Pet waste removal is a business that requires you to travel and work outdoors. Because of these considerations, there are several supplies you'll need to get started. Let's discuss the necessary equipment and why it helps you perform your job well.

A Smartphone

You likely already have a cell phone, but you might want to consider upgrading to a smartphone for your business. Smartphones have many useful features like GPS navigation, mapping programs, and more. Plus, having one on hand is also essential for communicating with customers via text or phone call. This business involves speaking to clients regularly and prospecting, so having a reliable smartphone can be beneficial.

Means of Transportation

Regardless of the size of your service area, you'll need a reliable way to travel from one client's home to the next. Because of this, owning a car or truck is ideal—mainly because you will carry around yard cleaning supplies and possibly bags of pet waste.

A Self-Contained Bucket or Debris Dustpan

You'll need a bucket or dustpan for scooping and collecting pet waste. Many pooper scooper business operators prefer self-contained buckets because they don't take up as much room in the vehicle and can be easily transported from place to place. Dustpans make it easy to collect a full yard of waste, without making repeat trips back and forth to the vehicle.

A Metal Pooper Scooper Waste Grabber

This tool makes it easier to reach pet waste in hard-to-reach spots, such as under bushes or decks. It also helps you avoid coming into direct contact with the waste. There are several variations of metal pooper scooper grabbers to consider—short, tall, and wired.

It's best to try out a few before settling on the one that works best for you. The one thing you don't want to compromise on is the metal material. Plastic doesn't scrape up pet waste as efficiently, especially on concrete.

A Shrub Rake and Blade Shovel

Both these tools are useful for digging out pet waste stuck in the grass. Sometimes organic material gets buried under the soil, and you'll need the right tools to get it out without damaging the lawn. You'll also want something durable for pushing and scraping the waste away.

13-Gallon Plastic Bags (or What's Required in Your Local Municipality)

You'll need bags to collect the pet waste from home to home before taking it to your disposal site. The bag size will depend on how much you intend to collect at each residential or business location. Typically, 13-gallon plastic bags are ideal for this work, but you may consider larger bags if you're collecting a lot of pet waste.

For example, you might need more oversized bags if you provide services for large-scale pet facilities. Before selecting a specific bag, it always helps to speak to your local waste disposal department to determine their regulations. While this is one of the ongoing business costs, buying in bulk can save money in the long run.

Bleach (for Sanitization)

You'll need to sanitize your scooping tools after each job, so having a bottle of bleach or other sanitizing agent on hand is invaluable. This will help eliminate harmful bacteria and keep your equipment clean between jobs. Mix water and bleach in a spray bottle to create a sanitizing solution. Paper towels can also be used to wipe down the tools and bucket before storing them.

Rubber Gloves and Boots

Safety should always come first when handling pet waste, so investing in gloves and boots to protect your hands and feet is essential. Disposable rubber gloves can be bought at most drugstores or online retailers. When it comes to boots, you want something waterproof, slip-resistant, and durable enough to last through any weather condition you might encounter.

Sun Protection (Eyewear & Hat)

If you plan on spending long hours outdoors scooping pet waste from yards, you'll need the right type of eyewear and sun protection. Invest in clear glasses or safety goggles to protect your eyes from dirt and debris. Additionally, if you plan on being in the sun for extended periods, a wide-brimmed hat can provide shade and keep your head cool. While you might assume sunglasses are ideal for summer weather, locating pet waste with them is challenging.

LED Headlamp (for Dark Weather)

When bad weather rolls in, you'll need a reliable light for locating pet waste. A headlamp with you can also be helpful if clients require early-morning services when the sun has not risen. Most LED headlamps come with adjustable bands that are comfortable enough to wear while scooping up yard debris. This frees up your hands to handle scooping tools and pet waste bags.

Bug Spray

Finally, bug spray is essential for pooper scooper business owners looking to limit their exposure to flying insects, such as mosquitoes and flies. Chemical and natural sprays are available for purchase at your local drugstore. Natural bug sprays also contain citronella, which can help ward off other pests like wasps and bees.

These items will help you get started in the world of professional pooper scooping, allowing you to make $300 or more daily! With the right supplies, there's no reason you can't begin a successful pet waste removal business today. Now that you know what type of equipment you need, let's discuss one more vital element—your uniform.

PLANNING YOUR UNIFORM

The most crucial equipment consideration for pooper scooping is your uniform. Not only does a uniform protect your body from the elements and potential hazards, but it also provides an opportunity for marketing and professionalism.

The type of clothing you wear will largely depend on the weather conditions in your local area. For hot and dry climates, light safety t-shirts with shorts or long-sleeve shirts with full-length pants are recommended to help protect against yard plants and pests. Hoodies, vests, and bodywarmers can act as a protective jacket when needed.

If you work in an area with wet and cold weather, your uniform requirements will be more extensive. Usually, the area is dark, which means drivers and pedestrians might not be able to see you unless you go with high-visibility safety clothing.

High-visibility clothing includes materials that are yellow, orange, or yellow-green. Retroreflective material is best for early morning and night work because it reflects light to its source. Fluorescent, reflective, and high-contrast materials can also work well in these conditions.

Opt for tri-blends, dry-blends, and 50/50 fabrics when selecting fabric for your uniform items. These materials help with moisture and can be easily screen printed or stitched with company information. Adding your logo or text like "Pet Waste Removal" on your uniform helps increase client visibility and recognition.

Jackets and pants with thermal layers are great for providing comfort and warmth during the cold months. Warm wear safety shirts and pants with a warm layer like fleece, coveralls, and thick coats will provide additional protection against the elements.

Whatever style you choose for your uniform, ensure it is comfortable enough for all-day use while still providing the protection needed to perform your job duties safely. Bright colors ensure that you're visible to clients and passersby. Remember, a well-designed uniform will be your best advertisement in the long run.

Having the correct uniform is critical for pooper scoopers. It provides a professional look and extra protection against pet waste, weather conditions, yard chemicals, and more. With the proper equipment in place, you can be sure of a successful venture into the world of pet waste removal.

Now that you understand how to form a business, the equipment you need to begin, and the uniform you'll wear, let's discuss the actual job of scooping doodies. The more efficiently you scoop, the more money you can make. Let's learn how to scoop yards efficiently and ensure dog safety at the same time.

ROUTINE DOODIES

There are two significant parts of being a pet waste remover that will make the job easier: scooping and safety. Knowing how to efficiently scoop yards is one of the most critical elements in pet waste removal success. Pet safety is also necessary because it protects you, the pet, and the customer. Let's cover both aspects to prepare you to do the job right.

How to Efficiently Scoop Yards

The nice thing about scooping yards is that the process is straightforward. With that in mind, there might be a few things you need to take care of before your first job. Here's the complete process to follow:

Set Up Your Scooping Tools

This includes gathering necessary items such as gloves, a pooper scooper, bags, and extra supplies like pick-up sticks. You can also line your dustpan with a plastic bag for easy disposal. Considering everything you need from the beginning helps you avoid running back and forth to the car for supplies.

Find the Poop

When scooping a yard, its important to find all the poop. You never want a client to walk outside and step in something that has obviously been missed.

We have found that the most efficient technique is to walk a tight zig zag across the yard. Start at one corner, and end at the opposite. You may want to walk the yard again but in the opposite direction if the yard has high grass.

Bag the Poop

Once you have all of the poop in your scooper, dump it into a bag (if you're scooper doesn't already have bag liners) and seal with a knot. If your client has agreed, you can simply place your bag into their outside bin. If not, you'll need to place the bag into a small trash can or plastic bin in your vehicle. If the bag and container are sealed, you shouldn't be dealing with any terrible odors if cleaned out after each shift.

Clean the Equipment

After picking up all the waste, rinse off your pooper scooper with a hose or water bucket and bleach solution. By properly cleaning your equipment between jobs, you avoid spreading any germs or diseases to other yards.

DOG SAFETY

It's essential to have a policy in place when dealing with pets during pet waste removal services. Asking clients to keep their pets indoors on visit days is one way to ensure everyone's safety. This issue may become relaxed as you scoop yards and get to know clients and their doggies, but you don't want to be responsible for an open gate or a dog escaping and possibly getting injured. Accidents happen and its best to take all proper precautions to ensure they don't during your cleaning.

Remind Clients to Keep Pets Indoors During Service Days

The best way to avoid any interaction with pets is to ask clients to keep their pets inside for the duration of your visit. Since most pet owners are understanding and compliant, this could be an easy solution. You can do this by sending a text reminder or confirming the appointment via email.

Avoid Any Chained Dogs

If you come across a chained dog, it's best to avoid any interaction. Never approach or touch a chained animal because it could become aggressive. While you might want to be friendly and offer the dog a treat, for instance, it's unsafe. Consider rescheduling with the client if this is the case.

Stand Still and Stay Quiet When Faced with an Unfamiliar Dog

If a dog approaches you, don't panic. Instead, stand still and stay quiet until the animal leaves. If it stays close to you, yawn or use a dog whistle, if available, to signal that you are not a threat. Make sure not to make eye contact to prevent the dog from becoming aggressive.

Follow these guidelines for efficient and safe pet waste removal services. The key is to be prepared, focus on the task, and never forget to clean your equipment. By following these steps, you can ensure that each job is done correctly and safely.

Whenever uncomfortable with a situation because of a pet, always take extra precautions and reschedule with the client. Following these tips can help you stay safe while providing excellent customer service.

HOW TO PRICE

There are several pricing strategies that business owners use to establish prices for pet waste removal services. Depending on your area and the services you offer, you can decide what works best for your business. These strategies will help you set prices that are profitable, while also competitive in your area:

Review What Other Businesses Are Charging

Researching the rates that competitors in your area charge for pet waste removal services is essential. This will help you set prices to match or slightly beat what other businesses offer. Doing this will also help you stay competitive in your market while making a profit.

Ask Prospects What They'd Be Willing to Pay

You can also ask potential clients what they're willing to pay for pet waste removal services. This will help you understand how much your target demographic is willing to pay, so you can set a price that makes sense with the market and your costs. If you're worried that you don't know who to ask, that's alright. In the next section when we cover marketing, you'll have plenty of ideas on how to reach potential customers.

Charge for an Initial Clean-Up

When starting, it's recommended to charge around $45 - $50 for an initial clean-up. This will give you a good idea of the size of the property and the amount of work involved in providing pet waste removal services. Whenever you onboard a new client, it's best to do an initial clean-up and switch to the pricing model we'll discuss next.

Charge for Weekly Service

The real income comes from providing repeat business. That's why it's important to offer weekly service at a rate of $15 per visit or $60 per month. This will give you steady income and the ability to provide quality services on a regular basis.

Up-Charge for More Than One Pet

If your clients have more than one pet, consider up-charging them for each additional animal they own. This will ensure that you're making enough money to cover your costs, while still being competitive in the market. While you may only charge a few dollars for additional pets, these small amounts add up quickly.

Up-Charge for Larger Yards

If your client has a large yard, it makes sense to up-charge them since there is more work involved in providing pet waste removal services. Depending on the size of their property, you might want to charge an additional fee for each extra acre that needs to be maintained. When you complete an initial cleaning, you can determine how much up-charging is appropriate.

Up-Charge for Emergency Cleans

If your client requires an emergency clean, you can up-charge them since they likely need the service immediately, and you're providing a valuable convenience. The price you set for emergency cleans should fall within the cost of an initial cleanup or one-time scoop.

While it might seem unlikely that customers pay for emergency cleans, the truth is that some of them will be willing to pay for the extra convenience. There are plenty of situations where they'll want to get the job done quickly, and you can provide that convenience.

Reduce Pricing for More Frequent Visits

You can also reduce pricing if a client wants more frequent visits. This will help ensure that you're still making enough money while offering a great deal to clients who need regular pet waste removal services.

Consider Business Costs, Such as Waste Disposal

Finally, make sure to consider all your business costs when setting pricing. Not only do you have to account for labor and overhead expenses, but you must think about the cost of disposing of pet waste. If you must pay for disposal services, factor that in when setting prices to stay profitable.

BUILDING AN ONLINE PRESENCE

Establishing an online presence is a must for any business. You want potential clients to be able to find and learn about your services, so here are the recommended platforms for a pooper scooper business.

Google My Business

Google My Business is a basic local search engine optimization service that establishes your services on Google Maps search results. This will help you show up when people in your area search for pet waste removal services. To set up GMB, you'll need to create a profile and verify it with Google by sending them a postcard with a verification code.

It helps if you have a public business address, web presence, and phone number associated with your Google My Business profile. When possible, it's also helpful to add reviews from satisfied customers to help potential clients find and trust your services. Regularly ask clients to provide feedback about your services and positively respond to negative reviews.

Facebook & Instagram

By establishing a presence on social media platforms like Facebook and Instagram, you can directly reach out to pet owners in your area. You can join pet-related groups or even create posts about the need for pet waste removal services. Creating a business page on Facebook and connecting with people in your area can also be a great way to find customers and build relationships with potential clients.

Facebook Marketplace is also applicable when trying to reach local clients looking for a pooper scooper business in their area. With this platform, you can advertise your services and target local clients needing pet waste removal. Try posting in local yard sale groups or city or suburb local groups. Always be sure to check their advertisement rules before posting, though. Between Facebook Groups, your page, and the Marketplace, you can create an effective online presence to draw in clients.

Instagram is great for creating beautiful visuals that showcase the importance of removing animal waste and showcasing before and after photos of jobs you've completed. Use hashtags and post regularly to gain more visibility. You should regularly add other pet-related content and promote your services by offering discounts or promotions.

Thumbtack or Nextdoor

Thumbtack and Nextdoor are two other platforms you can use to reach out to pet owners in your area. While Thumbtack is a platform that matches service providers with customers, Nextdoor is an online community for neighborhood-specific conversations.

Using Thumbtack, you create a profile of your services and add any relevant information like certifications or licenses, pricing structure, availability, etc. You can also request reviews from satisfied customers so potential clients know they're working with someone reputable.

Nextdoor is a great way to connect with local pet owners and build relationships with them. With this platform, you can join pet-related discussions, meet new people aware of the need for pet waste removal, and grow your presence in the local community.

While you don't need to have a presence on all these platforms, it's essential to establish a solid online presence, at least using Google My Business and social media sites like Facebook and Instagram. This will help ensure that people in your area know your services and can easily find them when they need pet waste removal.

Apps like Nextdoor and Thumbtack help you reach new customer bases actively looking for service providers. If you have trouble gaining enough customers through social media sites and local search engines, consider utilizing these platforms to reach out and spread the word about your pooper scooper business.

Additionally, most of these platforms allow paid advertising, which should be considered as you begin to grow your business. Paid advertising can be a great way to reach new customers and draw in more leads, especially if you are starting out. With that in mind, let's cover how you can acquire your first customers and generate $300 a day with your pooper scooper business.

ACQUIRING CUSTOMERS

One of the biggest starting hurdles to overcome when establishing a pooper scooper business is finding the clients who need your services. However, after you use even a few of these methods while advertising your competitive pricing, gaining customers shouldn't be a problem.

Running Ads

Ads are an effective way to reach potential customers in your area. Google AdWords allows you to target local people who have used keywords related to pet waste removal or pooper scooping services. The great thing about Google AdWords is that you can measure your ads' success and adjust them accordingly for better results.

Facebook and Instagram also offer great advertising opportunities by targeting users based on their interests. These social media platforms allow you to quickly reach out to pet owners who might need a pooper scooper service in the future.

Additionally, running ads in local newspapers is still a great way to get the word out about your business and ensure people know your services are available. Although you might think that no one reads papers anymore, you'd be surprised by how many people do and are looking for local services. Plus, many newspapers have online editions, which you can use to reach more people.

Posting in Groups

Facebook and Instagram groups can be a great way to connect with pet owners that might need your services. You can find groups related to pets, pet ownership, or even specific breeds of animals. These are ideal places to post pictures, offers, and other content to draw attention to your business.

When joining these groups, make sure you read the rules carefully and don't spam the members with blatant advertisements. Instead, offer helpful advice related to pet waste removal solutions or tips on keeping their yards clean. When you have something valuable to share with the group, they'll be more likely to pay attention and consider hiring you for their own needs.

As you become a recognized resource for pet owners in the groups, you can start to build relationships with them. With this platform, you can join pet-related discussions, meet new people aware of the need for pet waste removal, and grow your presence in the local community. After a few conversations, pitch your services and offer discounts to group members. It won't take long for your phone to start ringing with inquiries.

Networking

Networking is one of the oldest yet most effective ways to meet new people and acquire customers for your pooper scooper business. You can attend pet-related events and introduce yourself to potential customers as a pooper scooper service provider. Additionally, look out for online events related to the pet industry—these are often free or low-cost and a great way to meet new people who need your services.

When networking, make sure you have some materials that explain what your business does and how it can help them with pet waste removal needs. It's also important not to be too pushy when speaking with potential customers; instead, remain professional, knowledgeable about the subject matter, and confident that you can provide excellent service.

If there are any service provider groups in your area, this is a great way to connect with others in the pet industry and find potential customers. Showcase what makes you unique and highlight the value that you provide. When you're prepared to do business, be sure to close the deal with a solid handshake and exchange contact information. You never know how far networking can take your business until you try it.

Cold Calls

Cold calling is another powerful tool for acquiring customers for your pooper scooper business. With cold calls, you can reach out to pet owners who haven't heard about your services yet and explain why they need them. Make sure to have a script prepared before making any calls so that you know exactly what to say when talking to potential clients. Also, research numbers carefully-- many people will not answer random calls from unfamiliar numbers.

We recommend cold calling for business that could possibly use your services. Think vet offices, doggie daycares or spas, or pet stores that allow animals inside.

Door Hangers

Door hangers are an effective form of advertising, especially if pet owners in your area need your services. You can design door hangers to look professional, include a catchy phrase, and offer discounts for first-time customers. Door hangers will be visible without intruding on anyone's day or invading their space, making them an effective way to spread the word about your business.

Direct Mail

Direct mail is a great way to reach potential customers who haven't heard about your business yet. You can use direct mail campaigns to advertise special offers or introduce people to what you do. Direct mail pieces also allow you to incorporate visual elements into your message that might grab someone's attention and make them more likely to inquire about your pooper scooper services.

Unlike with door hangers, which don't require addresses, direct mail campaigns require that you have a list of addresses to target. You can find and purchase mailing lists from companies specializing in providing them or research and compile your own list by looking into public records like property tax databases.

No matter which method you use to acquire customers for your pooper scooper business, the key is to be consistent, creative, and relentless in your efforts. Try one or two marketing types, test their effectiveness, and determine whether or not it's working for your business. As you become profitable and want to scale up your business, you can add new marketing strategies and adjust existing ones to ensure you reach the right customers.

ACCEPTING PAYMENTS

After working hard to locate customers and offering to provide services to them, you need to be able to accept payments from them. Depending on your customer's preferences, there are different options available.

The most common payment methods include cash, check, card, and online payments. Which one you choose depends on the type of customer, their payment preferences, and your business needs.

Cash Payments

Cash payments are great for customers who have cash on hand or prefer to pay in cash. Cash is a reliable form of payment that is simple and easy for both customers and businesses alike. However, keeping track of cash transactions can be challenging and risky for small businesses because most people today don't keep cash around, opting for their preferred payment method instead.

Check Payments

Yes, some people keep checks around too, and businesses can accept payments in the form of a check. It's a reliable form of payment that allows customers to pay directly from their bank account.

However, it takes some time for the funds to clear, plus there is always the risk of bounced checks, so you should always be sure to check with your customer and confirm they have sufficient funds before accepting a check.

The good thing about check payments is there are no deposit fees. Yet, collecting checks after providing scooping services can be a challenge. Because of this, you may want to consider other payment options.

Card Payments

Card payments offer convenience for customers who prefer to pay with plastic instead of cash or checks. You can easily set up card reader machines or use an app on your mobile device—both are secure and easy-to-use options that can help you process payments quickly.

Just make sure you understand all the associated fees and regulations related to using these payment methods before proceeding. Generally, every transaction you make has a set percentage cost and a flat rate.

Online Payments

For customers who prefer to pay online, setting up an online payment system can help make the payment process more efficient. Many companies offer online payment solutions, such as PayPal and Venmo, which allow customers to pay with their debit or credit cards securely—and you can even set up subscriptions so customers can be charged automatically on a recurring basis.

Additionally, you may want to consider adding functionality to your website so customers can make payments directly from your site. If you built a WordPress site, adding payment provider options is as simple as installing a plugin. Website builders like

Wix and Squarespace also offer payment solutions that are compatible with their platforms.

However, you can expect to pay a higher monthly price to add this functionality to your current monthly website subscription, including additional processing fees. Yet, for the added convenience of automating customer payments and the flexibility it gives customers, this might be the right move for your business.

Mobile Payments

Finally, mobile payments can be an excellent option for businesses on the go. Mobile payment systems make it easy to accept payments anywhere and at any time. Popular options include Apple Pay and Google Pay; these are secure and efficient ways to process customer payments with minimal setup required. However, like card payments, there are associated processing fees that you should be aware of before using these solutions.

Understanding the various payment methods available and associated costs is essential when determining which options are best for your business. Additionally, researching different payment providers can help you better understand their features and advantages so you can choose the best fit for your customer base.

Here are some options to consider if you want to make either online or in-person payments, either during an initial cleanup or for recurring services:

PayPal

If you've ever done online shopping, you've probably used PayPal. This trusted payment provider lets customers pay with their bank account, credit card, or debit card—and it's accepted in more than 200 countries and regions.

Venmo

Owned by PayPal, Venmo is a mobile payment service that allows customers to send payments with just a few taps on the app. It's ideal for businesses that provide services and goods online since there are no setup charges or monthly fees. There are business accounts that you can easily establish, which give you access to 24/7 customer service and additional tools like invoicing.

QuickBooks Payments

QuickBooks Payments is an integrated payment processing solution from Intuit, the company behind QuickBooks accounting software. It allows businesses to accept major credit cards and ACH payments securely through its platform. What's nice about this option is that it ties into QuickBooks as a business and personal tax solution, saving you time and energy when managing your business finances and your taxes.

Square

Square is one of the most popular mobile payment systems available today. It's a payment processor, point-of-sale system, and digital wallet all in one—and it's accepted at over two million retailers worldwide.

Square stands out because of its point-of-sale software that can be used with any device, including smartphones and tablets. Therefore, if you want to accept in-person and online payments, you can easily do so with Square.

Ultimately, your chosen payment method or provider should depend on your business needs and customer preferences. Consider features, fees, security, and convenience when deciding which option is best for you and your pooper scooper business.

DEALING WITH INCLEMENT WEATHER

Working outdoors eventually means that you'll deal with bad weather. It can cost working hours and ruin schedules. Although you can recover from delays, consecutive days of inclement weather can impact your business. With proper planning and a little foresight, you can minimize disruptions and complete cleanups without interruption.

So, which steps can you take during seasons with potentially lousy weather? First, consider a four-day workweek that allows for Friday to be a make-up day in case it rains, snows, or the temperature drops too low. This lets you stay on track with your schedule and finish customer cleanup.

Additionally, be upfront about your policies with inclement weather in agreements and speak to clients about this problem. It would be best to keep them informed so they know what to expect during the cleanup process. Keep everyone in the loop by sending emails or text messages with updates as needed or by sharing statuses on your website and social media accounts.

When dealing with inclement weather, it's also essential to use your time wisely. Make use of these days by catching up on administrative tasks like accounting, marketing, or paperwork that are typically pushed to the side when you're busy scooping poop. This way, your business can remain productive while staying safe during inclement weather.

How to Plan Around Inclement Weather

The number one way to deal with inclement weather, besides having a backup plan using the above methods, is to use a top-notch schedule. Organizing your schedule ahead of time will help you plan around rainy or cold days.

For instance, if you know rain is likely in a specific week, adjust your schedule to accommodate it. This way, you can finish jobs faster and compensate for lost time due to the weather.

However, depending on your area, you might choose to work during particularly hot, cold, or rainy weather. Yet, there are some weather patterns you shouldn't ignore. For instance, if your area is prone to thunderstorms or high winds, it's best to alter your schedule accordingly. Your customers will understand and appreciate your caution in this matter.

For a moment, let's discuss planning your schedule around unexpected (and expected) weather events. The right online planner can help you stay organized and efficient while dealing with unexpected weather changes. Plus, even systems automatically email your customers to inform them of schedule changes or delays.

Lastly, use protective gear when needed. Although you'd have to spend extra money on raincoats and boots, it's worth the investment if it helps protect your health during bad weather. The right clothes and shoes will also help keep your customers' property clean in the rain, snow, or cold. It's critical to remember that when it comes to pet waste, safety is of utmost importance.

Ultimately, inclement weather should not be a problem for your pooper scooper business if you plan ahead. With the right tools and strategies, you can easily stay organized and keep your customers informed while remaining safe during extreme weather conditions.

NAVIGATING CANCELLATIONS

Unsurprisingly, cancellations and no-shows happen in the pooper scooper business. But you don't necessarily need to meet customers face-to-face during each appointment. The services you provide, fortunately, don't have the same issue with no-shows as other businesses do.

For example, the rate of cancellations and no-shows in the sales industry is upward of 25%. Luckily, people who want pooper scooper services already see the value in it. If you follow the following steps, you can control your business schedule regarding cancellations.

For starters, take payments upfront and provide service when you say you will. This way, it's less likely that clients will forget about their appointments or cancel at the last minute. Have a set day and time for specific ongoing clients so they know when to expect you. Stick to this routine and add new clients to the schedule when needed.

Furthermore, notify customers of schedule changes and ensure they prepare access to their yards for a clean-up session. Many people lock their backyards typically or keep their pets outside, which can create an issue if you don't have access when you arrive. If it happens when you arrive, this is just a matter of miscommunication, so try your best to send reminders of your policies and make sure they know when you're coming.

Additionally, send out reminder emails about your policies before appointments and reschedule if needed. If possible, try planning your schedule ahead of time so you can easily adjust to changes in the weather or unexpected cancellations. To be as efficient as possible, plan your route. This way, you can make the most of your time when servicing multiple clients in a row.

You'll want to group clients in service groups depending on their location. With a tool like Google Maps, you can add several addresses and plan a route that saves you the most time. Plus, you'll save on gas, while building an efficient route you can repeat.

Lastly, have a backup plan in case of inclement weather or other occurrences that could affect your business. Yes, an emergency event could happen at any moment, but having a plan in place will help reduce the stress of unexpected changes.

By following these steps, you can control your schedule and avoid unnecessary cancelations. This way, you can keep your pooper scooper business running smoothly despite any environmental changes. The nice thing about this work is that the customers rarely cause the cancellation. So, with some planning and organization, you can be sure your business is well-prepared to tackle any situation.

VEHICLE ORGANIZATION

How you organize your vehicle for pet waste removal depends on the size of your vehicle and the type of services you're providing. If you use a bucket and shovel to pick up after pets, storing those items in an efficient space should be easy enough.

On the other hand, if you want to use professional equipment like a pooper scooper vacuum, consider investing in a van or pickup truck with enough cargo room for your supplies. You can also customize your truck bed with drawers, shelves, and cabinets to keep everything neat and organized. This will make it easier for you to grab what you need quickly and get the job done faster.

Another option is installing custom racks inside the cab of your vehicle to hold small tools like gloves, bags, rakes, and shovels. This way, everything is within arm's reach for easy access. No matter what type of vehicle you choose, make sure it's big enough to carry all the supplies required to provide pooper scooper services.

One thing that pet waste business owners do is purchase a flatbed trailer that can be towed behind their vehicle. This provides more cargo space and allows them to bring all the necessary supplies without worrying about running out of room. Plus, you can use the trailer to transport pet waste to the dump or compost site.

Finally, be sure to keep safety in mind each time you transport pet waste. If you're using a trailer, ensure it's adequately secured to your vehicle and that nothing can fall off the back. You'll also want to avoid leaving pet waste in your vehicle for long periods, as it can create a pungent odor and attract pests. Be sure to properly dispose of pet waste as a habit at the end of your workday.

By being organized and efficient in your setup, you can reduce the time spent looking for supplies or digging through drawers. This will help you stay on schedule and give customers a better experience overall. With these tips on vehicular organization, managing your pooper scooper business should be a breeze!

MAINTAINING EQUIPMENT

Since you use many disposable products, there isn't much maintenance to complete as a pooper scooper. However, the equipment you must maintain is critical to your work. To keep things running smoothly and ensure customer satisfaction, it's crucial to have a preventative maintenance schedule for your vehicle and any equipment you regularly use.

Before driving, you should inspect your vehicle to ensure everything is in working order. This includes checking lights, brakes, tires, and windshield wipers. Although it might seem excessive, you have a schedule to maintain, so the last thing you want is a broken-down vehicle causing delays. It would help if you also inspected your tools routinely to determine when equipment should be replaced. Doing so will help you avoid any accidents or mishaps that could endanger yourself or your customers.

Start by inspecting your tools routinely to determine when they should be replaced or need servicing. Set an alarm on your phone or calendar system, so you don't forget these necessary checks. Additionally, monitor your maintenance expenses to budget appropriately throughout each month and take stock of your disposable products. This way, you'll know precisely what needs replenishing and when.

It's also beneficial to buy subscriptions or regularly shop for the disposable items you use most often. This can help save time, money, and energy in the long run, so you don't run out of supplies frequently. With sites like Amazon offering subscription services, you can guarantee that you regularly receive the necessary items to keep your business running smoothly. Sign up for a subscription, and Amazon will ship more supplies directly to you at a predetermined date. This can make life much easier and ensure your pooper scooper business is always ready for the job!

Overall, having a well-maintained vehicle and equipment is essential for any pooper scooper business. With proper organization and maintenance, you can ensure that all your tools remain in working order and make the most of your workdays. Without focusing on your equipment, there will be a risk of delays, customer dissatisfaction, and other issues that can affect your bottom line. So, take the time to maintain your equipment and supplies regularly to keep your business running successfully.

GOING THE EXTRA MILE

Differentiating your services from other pet waste removal businesses takes your company to the next level. Providing additional services like cleaning trash cans, flower beds and holiday cards can create an impression of quality and help separate you from the competition. Small touches like this can create repeat customers and generate word-of-mouth referrals.

For example, providing holiday cards or free trash can cleanings for new customers could be an excellent way to stand out. You can also offer additional services like leaf removal and garden maintenance, especially during the spring or fall. Doing this will demonstrate that you are dedicated to your job and willing to go the extra mile for your clients.

The Importance of Customer Referrals

Word-of-mouth referrals are one of the most powerful tools you have when it comes to growing your business. Creating an excellent customer experience is essential for any pet waste removal service. Doing so will ensure customers feel appreciated and help create a positive environment around your services.

You should routinely check in with clients to ensure they're happy with your work and provide them with additional resources they may need. Customers who recognize that you're invested in their satisfaction are more likely to recommend your services to others.

Offering discounts or referral incentives is also beneficial, as this can effectively gain new clients quickly.

Reviews and testimonials from satisfied customers are great ways to spread the word about your business. Encourage customers to leave reviews on social media or other platforms to boost your visibility and gain the trust of potential future customers. That's right, word of mouth doesn't just happen in person anymore—your business strategy should also include digital referrers.

By focusing on providing exceptional service and winning referrals, you'll have enough business to keep your pooper scooper business busy year-round. If it seems simple enough, that's because it is! If you care for your customers, keep communication lines open, and always put in the extra effort, your business will thrive.

Why Customer Service is at the Core of Your Business

As a pooper scooper, customer service is the lifeblood of your business. Responding promptly to emails and phone calls, keeping a friendly attitude, arriving on time to jobs, and being mindful of customer privacy are all things that will help keep customers coming back. Additionally, offering pet waste removal services with an eco-friendly approach can show clients that you care about the environment and their community.

Your primary goal should always be customer satisfaction, so make sure to take complaints seriously and offer fair refunds or discounts when applicable. Additionally, you can use customer feedback to enhance your services and better meet the needs of pet owners. People love knowing that their opinions are being heard, so if they have a suggestion, take the time to listen and address any issues that arise.

By providing top-notch customer service and thoughtful extras, you can ensure your pooper scooper business stands out from the competition. Doing so will help bring in more customers and ensure success for your business. Regardless of how you choose to differentiate yourself, customer service is at the core of every pooper scooper business and should be taken seriously.

Excellent communication skills are also crucial for managing client relationships. Make sure to set clear expectations about your services upfront, so that clients know what to expect from you when it comes time for their pet waste removal. Building solid relationships with customers can help increase word-of-mouth referrals and, ultimately, your bottom line.

Overall, running a successful pooper scooper business requires an investment in time and effort. However, by focusing on the correct maintenance of equipment and supplies, going the extra mile to differentiate from competitors, and offering excellent customer service, you can ensure your pooper scooper business is always ready for the job!

CONCLUSION

Start Building a Successful Pooper Scooper Business

Phew! You just learned a ton of information about the ins and outs of starting a pooper scooper business. Developing a plan, assessing customer needs, investing in the right equipment, setting yourself apart from competitors, and providing top-notch customer service are all essential elements to running a successful business.

When it comes down to it, you'll need time and effort to make your pooper scooper business thrive—but with dedication and hard work, this could be the start of a gratifying career! Within a few months, you should easily hit your income target of $300 a day. By putting in additional work, you can even expand from one-time services to longer-term contracts and increase your profits.

While there will be plenty of situations to navigate, you'll be on your way to success with enough planning and the right attitude. It might seem incredibly difficult to gain your first customer, but it can be an incredibly satisfying business venture once you do. Persevere during challenging moments; before you know it, your pooper scooper business will thrive!

If any questions arise during your journey, revisit this resource, and use the other tools at your disposal. While not every question is addressed in books and online, reaching out to the right people can offer invaluable advice. It might not seem like people in your industry will want to help, but it might surprise you how many entrepreneurs are more than willing to lend a helping hand.

Good luck in your pooper scooper business endeavors—you've got this! With the right approach, you'll be a pro at poop scooping in no time. And who knows? You may even discover a newfound passion for picking up pet waste along the way! Happy scooping!

www.ingramcontent.com/pod-product-compliance
Lightning Source LLC
Chambersburg PA
CBHW070750220526
45467CB00018B/1898